# The Way Words Travel

Morelle Smith

Published by the UKA Press 2005

2 4 6 8 10 9 7 5 3 1



First published in Great Britain in 2005 by the

UKA Press

PO Box 109,
Portishead, Bristol. BS20 7ZJ

www.UKAuthors.com

A CIP catalogue record for this book is available from the British Library

ISBN 1-904781-46-2

This book was prepared for print by the
UKA Press

Cover Design by Peter J. Merrigan

ACKNOWLEDGEMENTS

In June 2003 I was invited to spend a month as Writer in Residence at Maison d'Emma, St Mathieu-de-Treviers, France. I would like to express my grateful thanks for this opportunity to devote time to my writing.

Some of these poems have previously appeared in *New Writing Scotland, Poetry Scotland, Poetry Monthly, Borderlines, Poetry Cornwall, The Eildon Tree, Fife Lines, After the Watergaw.* Thanks are due to the publications and editors.

*For Frieda and Matti*

# Contents

# The Rhythms of Time

*Edinburgh*

Sitting on the stone steps
at Bristow, one or two skateboarders
grinding and clicking
in the twilight.
The white lights flickered
behind leafless branches,
the paved area, trees
leaning over and a catch
in time's spinning
and turning, a pause
in its wheel from curving,
to stillness. Like a skateboarder,
time is at rest, to reflect
or to catch up with all
the movement that it left behind.
Dim lights, soft footsteps
in a still-winter night.
Tom and I share crisps and nuts.
I'm reluctant now, to stand up and go on,
to step back on time's trajectory,
its trolley time, its bus and flight time,
the moving airport walkway.
The evening stretches soft and limp -
the illusion of choice always
more seductive in the dark.

But we stand up,
head for the next frame -
the tuning of the instruments,
the music, wine and laughter,
and the presents people gave me.

It snows when I head out to the airport
and when I step onto the plane -
flakes of music
and splinters of remembered conversation
stick to my mind like burrs
until time speeds up again
and they fall into the eerie cloudscape
I'm flying over,
with its markings and patterns
as if some giant bird
has walked across the clouds
leaving footprints you would never see
from the shrouded, sun-starved
earth below.

I fiddle with the mind's controls,
playback and rewind -
familiar lyrics from the 'home' station,
pieces of foreign languages
I want to splice into my mouth
and gestures - my limbs and bloodstream
and the way I think.

Always this pursuit of something
that I know quite well
cannot be preserved or eaten,
cannot be absorbed so totally
that you become one with it forever.
For part of its allure is

that it's often just beyond
your fingertips - round the
next corner, over the next page,
framed in the next face,
born into the next sunrise,
arrived at in the next city
that the aircraft lands in.

The familiar tunes grow faint,
and more sporadic -
there is more static on the wavebands,
till reception fuzzes into
flicker, then a constant hiss.
The signal breaks up.
The foreign stations just remind you
that you lean on language
like a lover, like an arm
across your back.

## *Tirana*

I try to fit the new sounds
into music. Outside,
a dog barks. Then a loud banging
like someone hitting corrugated tin,
the kind that fits round
wooden stakes and looks as if
you could crumple it in your hand.
The squeal of a slipping fan-belt,
as a car goes past.

Morelle Smith

Two men in the street -
one beating a round drum -
one side with a stick,
the other with a flat switch,
so you get two different sounds.
My fingers twitch in sympathy,
remembering my drum.
The second plays a kind of clarinet -
reedy and rotating sound -
a wheel, rather than a scale,
that comes to rest.
No goals, no climaxes
and no crescendos.
I find time lurking here -
spinning and waltzing,
a kind of time I could hold hands with,
a time that's in movement
without being restless,
a time that is slow, but nimble-fingered,
that doesn't slow down or stop,
that barely pauses,
that has no predetermined
goals and agendas that must
be adhered to, come what may,
that moves more obliquely
than directly, that sidles
and saunters rather than
follows a straight line,
or the quickest route.

The musicians pass beneath
the window, disappear
round a corner, then return,
minutes later.
The rhythms can feel stifling,

or enfolding, like the circling
call of the muezzin,
the spiral can reach in
to a place you can remember,
like a blurred snapshot
of a childhood home -
but cannot place, because
whatever fixes memory in place
was absent; so there is just
a trace of something that's familiar -
a scent, a brief expression
on someone's face - an emotion
that you have no name for.

In the mornings, heavy thumps outside
are people banging carpets
against the balconies.
At night, you hear much louder bangs,
which you ignore.

'There are no roads in Albania,
only directions' someone says.
Today's direction wound
up Dajte mountain, looping and curving,
crumbling at the sides.
We abseiled down a sandy
rockface and looked out across the valley,
saw the distant Adriatic.
Driving back, pulled over
for a few cows, wearing halters -
passed a donkey with a wooden
saddle, standing still, untethered.
People at the roadside sell
yellow blossom, olive oil,
bananas and black seeds.

But tonight, flicking through
the channels, I found
that memory of sitting
at Bristow, on the stone steps,
sharing peanuts, with the soft
street lights outlining
the shape of a dancer
who's paused, to let all
the varieties of time
catch up with the present.
Yellow flowers, orange sand,
black seeds and honey-coloured oil.

Soldiers outside the government buildings,
dressed in black fatigues,
holding brown rifles,
have brown eyes and black hair
and they watch you as you walk past -
not with aggression or suspicion
but because they too
are caught up in the eddies
and the rhythm and
the patterns of time.

# Shkodra, February, Early Afternoon

There is no wind, in the dusty street.
No sound of cars, or human voices.
A cat slides across a roof,
a shadow, a discarded leaf.
Vines and curly trees twist round
posts and sticks and fences.
We are all waiting for the spring.

The sun is warm on our faces
but time is stretched out on the rooftops,
like the dogs in the hospital yard,
empty of desire.
A woman on the balcony across the street,
wears a blue dress, and sifts flour into a tub.
In the distance, the mosque dome
glitters in the sunlight.

When I get up, I walk quietly
as if there's something I'm reluctant
to wake up, I don't want to disturb.
I look back at the balcony,
at the woman standing at the tub of flour,
round sieve in her hand.
The street between us, painted
with yellow light.

Morelle Smith

What will happen if I tread
on time's toes, as it lies
stretched on the pastel roof tiles,
dreaming its private dreams
we can only feel and smell and guess at,
as the oranges ripen on the tree
outside the window?
I tell myself I'm not afraid
of time's interrupted sleep
or severed dreams
but I imagine - as I step back
from the balcony and sunlight,

into the darkened room -
that its newly-opened eyes
will be dark-brown, and its hand
softer than any time-worn
calloused hand should be.

# Early Evening, Downtown Tirana

A new Moon in the evening sky,
some blurs of pink above
the squat horizon.
Some parts of the pavement
are completely broken up;
other parts are level,
smooth new flagstones
set in careful cement, pink
and green and honey-coloured
hexagons. You tread
carefully on them,
savouring their shape and colour,
their precise alignment,
through your soles.

On stone benches by the trees,
on wooden boxes outside shops,
men play dominoes and chess.
Dust rises in the streets,
behind the cars.
The traffic rolls past slowly -
mostly long, mustard Mercedes
or the white land-cruisers
of international relief teams -
Red Cross, UNHCR,
*Médecins sans frontières*
(dubbed *médecins sans voitures*

in the north, because so many
vehicles were stolen).

Spring comes with a sudden
scent of flowers-
you can almost see Time loitering,
a hazy figure in the twilight
and the dust rising from the potholed streets,
strewn with stones and garbage
and an orange glow here and there,
from dying fires.

At night, when you walk
past the railings of the stadium
and the large van that is always parked there
with *'première urgence'* painted on its sides,
there is a small fire burning -
a few pieces of wood, red
embers. Sometimes there is
someone squatting by the fire;
often it just glows unattended,
by the railings,
underneath the trees.

# Epiros Nights

*(In classical times, what is now southern Albania was known as Northern Epiros)*

The smell of jasmine and orange blossom,
the kiosk selling apples, cigarettes
and chocolate; the balcony,
overlooking the sea.
Arnie's garden in Saranda,
where he waters plants;
historians and archaeologists
sit in the shade, talking of Illyria
and the lion gate at Butrint,
and a body that was washed up
on the shore.

The citadel museum at Gjirokaster
had a handful of Socialist Realist
paintings, a few traditional
sheepskin cloaks, old cannons,
a tank and a MIG plane
on the outside terrace.
On the roof, laced with
barbed wire, we looked through windows
to the prison cells below.
The caretaker called to us angrily -
we weren't supposed to go there.

Morelle Smith

The prison cells are empty now,
used in King Zog's time.
The Communist era is a gap
in memory - pilfered rifles
and abandoned heroes,
crossed-out faces and nothing
to replace them with.
Crowds of people standing in the street,
waiting for the visas
that will let them leave.
The mountains have a claim
on sky and the sun carves
shadows like black lace.

The race of sun across the sky
and the faces in the street,
heavy with waiting.
I buy postcards, sunglasses,
a cassette.
Eyes watch us, smooth as cobbles,
dark as shadow, as we drive
slowly past them down the narrow street.
The valley road runs north
and the mountains follow us.

Living in these mountains
must trap your dreams, I think,
in soft gullies that
stretch your fingers to breaking,
trying to prise them out.
Great gulfs of memories
are left behind.
Dreams turned into rocks.

Ballsh was like a prison camp -

dusty, broken, heaped with rubbish,
dirty, sullen.
Kavaje had cool, fringy palms
and soft lights from roadside kiosks.
Driving in the dark, you could not
see the potholes and we jumbled
through the night, bounced
and rattled through the stony paths.
The shabby streets of downtown Tirana
felt - almost welcoming,
almost - home.

Tonight, the thunder mutters,
then claps its cloudy hands.
The lightning flickers, like
a giant, electronic butterfly.

Ali Pasha's castle, on the Saranda road,
is utterly abandoned.
The gardens overgrown,
the roof a nest of weeds.
The sea glitters below,
a clear and lapis blue,
hinged with light.
The underground caverns are dark
and full of ghosts.
Epiros nights are full of the scent
of jasmine blossom.

# Albanian Sunday

The sound of church bells
catches the morning breeze -
and something cool and languid
and secure as heaven
drifts in with a wave of blossom scent
and cooking smells.

Later, the muezzin sounds
the call to prayer,
and you are wrapped around
with dusk, a yellow fingernail of moon
hangs over baking city streets.
Buildings are splashed with fiery red
and the moisture on your skin
has turned to gold.

# Positive Braking

Above the edge of balcony
city lights shiver;
a diesel engine turns over,
then drives off.
Faint music hisses treble
and a dog barks in the distance.
Someone from a place I still call home
calls me on the telephone.
I listen to a world that turns
and changes, events that pass
without me.

I think of the grasshoppers and crickets,
the dragonflies and little lizards,
the tortoises that stroll along
embankments - the weight of sun
and softness of the nights.
No ravines of emotion
no mountains in the mind,
and wonder if I'm looking
for an anchor or a foothold
or a simple memory
of something that I've left behind.

There is no breath of wind.
A shop-front shutter rattles down.
This morning, climbing over

the pilasters of the abandoned building,
rope around my waist;
my feet planted against the stonework -
I feel an exhilarating sense
of slippage, as I move my
hand out and the rope
rushes through the carabina
and I leave the stone
and briefly fall through space.
Those seconds of free-fall -
that I cannot remember.

'Let go with both hands'
the instructor said,
'push away from the wall and -
drop.'

# The God of Open Doorways

This metal morning, hung between
pink flecks of cloud,
and a moon that's growing crumply
at the edge, wilting like a dry
and curling leaf.
The high-pitched curve of swifts.

The psyche of this country, like the land,
is full of cliffs, ravines and precipices.
For all the space, there is a sense
of being folded and cocooned in rock.
The mind is terraced, like a vineyard,
with beliefs, running as deep as winter
in the frozen footsteps of the valley.

They lie in gorges, painted on rock walls,
reminding you of feelings
that do not belong to you.
You are a slip of their tongue,
you inhale only a flicker of this feeling
and it removes all solid ground.

After that, there is the sea -
roped and gemmed with light,
pale green and salty.
Holding you up, like time.
Swallowing you,

like time.

What god is tracking me?
Whether you go with it or resist,
whether you deny it, rush inside it,
revere it or cajole it,
it is there.

To be accepting of either outcome -
there's a thing.
To not cling, to what you want so much
to be the future.
To not need it to be one thing or the other.
What god is that?
The god of roads or open doorways?

Perhaps it is the salt god,
that floats you on the water.
Or the god that tends the garden,
pruning, weeding,
sweeping the dead leaves and branches.
He asks no questions.
He is very quiet.
He looks at you as you
walk through the entrance.
He notes the patterns that the sea
has made on you, the little
ridges and indentations,
the colours of the sky at dawn.

With the marks of the sea's fingers on you,
He leaves you free to wander
in this garden.

You watch the muscles in his shoulders
as he works
and you move closer to him.

# Tirana Park

Boys break-dancing,
crickets frisking air
like an overdue suspect.
Sheep crossing the path
and I've a cherry in my mouth,
dark-red cherry,
thinking of you, Patrice
when I bite into it.

A dragonfly circles round me hungrily.
I listen to the frogs at night,
and the lonesome john-john bird.
I listen to you too,
a pile of cherry stones around my feet,
sun skidding through the sky, behind the lake,
losing its footing, as it always does,
camouflaged in red, to throw night
off its track.

The light is just beginning to pack its bags,
to follow the sun - grumbling, just a little.
Bats flex their wings, restless.
Come on bats, let's get going -
the lizards have already found their rocks
to sleep under, and any lonely bats
can come with me
accompany this path-walker,

this trail-follower who is thinking of you.

Afflicted with this love of evening,
perhaps I could give you some of that,
as a silent bat swoops low across my shoulder.

# Leaving Albania

My mind is peeling away
from this place - separating,
like two sheets of paper.

Once, this place and I were stuck so close
together - your time pressed against me
like sun on my palm,
like a thumb,
like a hard coin,
like a hand or a whole other
body, like someone that you watch -
while he does not know that you are watching -
someone you listen to,
when he does not know
that you are listening and the sounds
of his voice run over your eyelids
like water, down your face and arms
and into your palm.

Your time was my time -
I wore you and my palm
was hot with your sun
and I wore you with
no distance and no separation.

But your time is leaving -
or perhaps it is mine -

peeling from me like purple fig-skin -
and the days tremble slightly,
and the roasted corn sellers grow
dim and less bright
with the scent of hot charcoal
and the hurrying nights
with their sackfuls of shade
smearing an ashy line between
kerbstone and road, between evening
and light; between your thumb
and my palm.

Crimson peppers, marine blue grapes,
dusky purple figs and lemons
so yellow I blink my eyes,
have a shawl of time on them,
marked by the lacy pattern
of the chestnut trees.
Time's hand is less pressing
but its mark rests on me
like a melody, a reedy music
that wanders up the thin streets,
doused with shade.

This place and me shared one time,
like lovers, we counted no costs
and no losses, the dusty streets
they were me, and the rocking paving
stones and the rubble were my wake
and my clouds and my forgetfulness.
My palm was the pressure of your thumb.

My mind is peeling away
from this place but the sun itself -
or so it seems -

has hesitated, and has not left yet.
If something called future
takes your thumb from my palm
what will I call you then?
Past?  A memory?  A dream?
And what will I call myself
when I have never felt as close
to time as I do
now.

# Jardin en Mouvement

From Javel Metro station,
I cross the road,
close to the river,
pass a deserted brasserie -
it is a cloudy morning,
with a faint wind,
and it is early yet -
and walk along the rue Balard.
At the entrance gate
to the garden of Andre Citroen
there is a sign
to say it is permitted
to walk upon the grass.

The garden is very quiet.
It is listening.
It seemed cold at first,
impersonal, measured, angled,
laid out with a sense
of strict control.

At the far end, across an area
as empty as a sports pitch -
there are tall glass buildings,
mirroring roofs and trees and sky
with a reflective and distorting eye.
Across the Seine, on the *rive droite*,

a block of flats, stained balconies,
colours peeled and cracked with time.

But on the other side, I find
*le jardin argent* and *le jardin doré*
and the sun comes out, wedging itself
between two clouds.
Then the bamboo leaves shake,
thin, Andean music, fragile pipes -
delicious laughter, on the border
between sound and light.
Something in me floats upwards
and I walk on light, not grass.

In *le jardin vert* there were
giant hogweed; in this part,
huge yellow flowers with fat and
sprawling leaves mix with the
giant thistles.
Leaves turn plum purple at the
fringe of trees.

Even this wild place is 'authorised' -
but, allowed, it flourishes,
it speaks and it lays shadows
gently on the ground.
It is not afraid of strangers
and does not try to hide itself.
It revels in attention, this yellow,
moving garden, hooks itself
on you, the rose thorns,
and the candelabra branches
of the thistles.
I take off my sandals, touch the grass
with the skin of my feet

and the sun burns like a dragon
in this morning heat and I lie back
on the wooden seat and feel the grass -
hot as stone
and soft as river water,
underneath my feet.

# Remember

Smells of garlic from a basement
in the New Town.
It is evening, and the light
has settled like a skin.
Tree-shadows shift and stir
the edges of this light,
colours deepen,
light grows thicker,
and the pavements are still warm.

*Remember the swifts in the garden*
*at Sevres?*
*And the wooden blocks in* le jardin argent,
*step-sized, to walk across*
*the floating lily pads?*
*The olive leaves were the colour*
*of thick cloud polished*
*with unshed rain.*
*I changed at Michel Ange Molitor*
*to go to the garden*
*of Andre Citroen.*

On the sky-line tonight
there's a curve of a building,
a glass wing, reflecting the sky.

*Remember the pinnacle buildings*

*around La Defense? Mute,*
*some layered like terraces,*
*mirroring sky, their reflections*
*curved and distorted,*
*magnified, buckled - these buildings*
*see with Cubist eyes.*
*The echoing walkways,*
*The sculpture of The Sleepwalker -*
*poised on this round ball,*
*about to step off*
*and you catch your breath*
*but his bronze balance*
*is perfect.*
*Further on, in a large square*
*of water, black metal rods*
*are hung with coloured lights.*
*There is language behind*
*this glass and metal skin.*
*But it's muffled, distorted.*

*Is it saying - set me free?*
*Or is it saying - let me in?*

Close to the river, trailing willows
and poplar trees and home of morning
heron gliding -
there are spice-smells -
dahl and jeera,
coconut and cardamon
and coriander.
It's almost dark now.

*It was dark when we reached*
*the cafe de Thym,*
*in the rue St. Martin.*

Morelle Smith

*The actor in the white T-shirt*
*and trousers with braces*
*talked of St. Exupery,*
*and outside - the rain.*
*The cars move slowly,*
*wipers splashing, and the rain*
*falls on our faces,*
*in the rue St. Martin.*

*On sunny evenings there were*
*cafe tables spilling onto pavements,*
*and red wine*
*and Metro station names like*
*rue du Bac, Iena, Solferino,*
*Javel, St. Paul, la Bastille -*
*but we remember them in rain,*
*always the rain,*
*spilling down our faces.*

The scent of white roses
in St. Vincent St.
Do you remember?

# Mucha Lady

(for John Renbourn; after visiting Alfons
Mucha's exhibition at La Trocadero, Paris)

Mucha lady,
head tilted,
coils of abandoned hair
like a resting wind
with memories of travel.
Her smile is not for you,
It's for herself.
Who could not love her?

You pared your fingernails,
wrote squiggly notes
on music paper.
In the Orangerie
I caught you looking at me
from a doorway.

Mucha lady,
head tilted backwards
in delight.
You might envy her,
desire her,
but who could not love her?

You sharpened pencils

as I drove south;
the scent of shaved wood
and graphite mixing
with the smell of
February rain.

Driving through Toulouse in darkness
we spent the night in Foix.
You brought out your guitar,
tinkered with knots and rags
of tune and said -
'I'm going to call this Languedoc
or maybe even -
Mucha Lady.'

# Rue des Grenouilles, St. Mathieu

"Just to be held by the ocean
is the best luck we could have"
*Rumi*

Because of just the small amount of rain last night,
the green pond has a hint of murky turquoise.
It has expanded to twice its size.
The dragonflies, enormous, choose the tips
of long green reeds to balance on -
blue notes on a green score -
and these reeds sway up and down
like the wind may sway you,
like the way the ocean might just hold you -
if you are very lucky.

A frog shifts from its resting-place
of wood or stone, plumped up with fuzzy green -
and it swims off slowly, upstream,
to the shade the bridge casts,
doing frogstroke, till it's out of sight.

# Lack of Net

I wander through the marketplace,
fingering bright oranges
and the sharp edges of the leaves
of artichokes.
I'm looking for something to save me,
to catch my fall.
I remember touch and how
that saved me then, but not now,
not in memory. I walk hungrily
through the market, scratched and soothed
with memory, and oranges,
and the scent of sun-warmed
pine needles.

There is no safety net,
and yet this swift descent
into the touch and texture
of the emptiness and depth
and void of me, is all I am,
and the darkness of it
rustles the leaves gently,
like the wind.

I cannot explain how this
deep pain, and lack of net
to catch me,
turns into something else -

as if what we have most to gain from
always slips the net -
and we fear it more than anything.

When you feel that fear come up in you
you can only walk towards it with all your
social masks of looking good and being seen
to look good and confident, successful,
sophisticated, witty, wise, intelligent,
with important things to do -
tossed in the rubbish bin, as you
walk towards your fears.

The train squeals slowly to a halt,
at the Gare de l'Est.
I remember the market,
the dresses and shoes,
the melons, smooth-skinned and
canary yellow - rough-skinned
and pimpled, grey-green,
rounded rock-surfaces, flooding
my fingertips with memories
I held inside me, that
I did not know I had -
fingertips stumbling with love,
over the gently pitted melon
surface - hesitant with love
over that other skin -
soft and almost edible -
but I do not remember
who I am, no,
I am burdened with a sense
of fear - that I will be exposed,
found out, that all my hidden
longings, covered by this bright

and confident facade, will be exposed,
as clearly as if I peeled off
garment after garment,
and I walked naked through the crowds
along the Boulevard Sebastopol.

But there are other secrets too -
like the one of who we really are -
which I suspect is carried
by a being who walks as close
to me as possible - and sometimes
that is far away, because I do
not let him near me.
Until the illusion of something
that will save me drops away
and the earth itself turns liquid
and I fall and fall -
and weep for loss of something
I cannot hold onto,
and for the falling feeling,
the abyss of who I thought
I was.

I am lack of net, he whispers
to my bruised and shaken body,
and I have been waiting long,
so long, to be with you,
and to let you know that
this embrace is who you
really are.

Sunlight hits the thick, green
water-soup of the canal St Martin,
throws insanity of kisses
on my skin.

I sit down on a bench,
whispered by the honey-scent
of the platanes.
I weep a little, for the joy of it,
the homecoming of it,
the speckled sunlight
and the cobbles and the car horns
and the rattle and the screech
of metal over metal
as the trains come overground
onto the metal bridges
and stop at Stalingrad.

The canal goes on, towards the Seine,
but I turn right at Oberkampf,
and walk the streets, with
their carpet-slices of sun,
their lemon-cake layers,
to the rue du Temple,
last seen in winter damp,
and now, blossomed with light.

Morelle Smith

# Redonner Le Rêve

Tu m'as redonné-
Comme on offre une cigarette
Ou un café
Comme si tu le portais dans ta poche
En attendant notre rencontre -
Mon chemin et l'avenir,
Inaccessible
A ce moment, a ce présent,
Mais dont je peux rêver.
Tu m'as redonné
Mon rêve.

# Cityscape

The River Café. Solid wooden tables,
Mugs of coffee, croissants,
Raisin scones and jam.
Later, we walk by the river
And a street which empties
And shivers suddenly with silence -
As can happen sometimes in the city.
Just past *Le Marche Noir,*
My voice dropped to a whisper,
Not to disturb the silence.

A group of birds - blackbirds
Or starlings, five or six, were perched
On the very top of a pointed tree
As if they had to get as
High up as they could.

A small tree sprouted from
A disused doorway.
Half a brick, a cracked flower-pot,
A piece of plaster broken off,
Two coils of rusted wire,
All left behind. And the tree,
Which is just beginning.

# Citta Bella

They scrape your heart,
these half-demolished buildings,
walls like murals,
with empty patches
remembering fireplaces,
red brick rectangles
reminding of windows,
exposed to any passing stranger's gaze,
whether curious, indifferent,
judgmental or careless -
do you still love me?
that's what I hear them say.
Yes, I whisper, walking past,
remembering windows
and delicacies of the vision,
savoured in silence or twilight
and its mad mixture of colours over rooftops,
a crumb of croissant on my upper lip
a dream of elsewhere on my upper eyelid.

Trains going past,
coming out of a tunnel -
steps down to the road.
Rainfall on city streets.

Colin's voice drowned out
by a truck revving round

the corner.

Sudden peals of bells
from Greyfriars church
entering the classroom
throwing holy water
on Xiaouli's description
of the Chinese population.
Jose writes the 0's
on the blackboard and they
trail downwards.

Is he optimistic? asks Jean-Louis
and the church bells toll
and fade and swing and
urgently come through the window
while we wrestle with nothings
and the chalk scrapes on the
blackboard and the bells
toll summer and warm air
and a timeless place
and I look out onto the cemetery
and the classroom disappears
in this measured, urgent,
endless sweep of sound.

# Dervish Dancer

You're my blur, that edge
between my fingers and my mind.
You linger in the inner eye,
selected moments, highlights
from the cameraman
and soundman, the musicians
and the film crew
I carry round with me.
They've selected shots of you -
not the ones I chose, but -
I admire their angles, the way
they caught you
when you were not looking.

You stroll through my tree-lined
avenues that remind me sometimes
of the Champs Elysees and
Rue St Martin and at other times
of leafy Sami Frasheri
and Vaso Pasha.

Like the albatross, living its life
in flight, you touch down
rarely, and the memory of skin
and the tactile rhythms of your
speech throb in my blood
like an exotic dance,

a Roma incantation.
Looking for the dervish dance,
the ultimate, where you will be
translated into language
that your tongue has never spoken,
but you know as your true home.

# Grey Sky

(for Angus Calder)

All the sky-colour has drifted
down to the horizon; a blot,
a fold, rumpled sky-skin
layered on hill-tops.
Grey has many colours in it -
the blue of smoke, purplish
at sundown, early morning
green and storm yellow.
Grey is only packed light
folded like stacked sheets,
sky's messy bedroom,
its abandoned clothes.

# Hay-On-Wye

Outside a cafe -
parasols over plastic tables
on uneven cobbles
I put down my bag of books
and the guy at the next table says -
watch out - your parasol might
fall off - mine just did.
Seeking shade from this hot,
and unexpected sun.

Rooks calling in an English garden -
red-brick houses and deep peace -
lily-pads in the little pond -
tiny frogs and lush delphiniums.
Thick light spread in a
pasty haze over hedge-hugged
hills, this morning.
No fortressed churches here,
no defensive buildings and no fear
of invasion.
Only rumours, now deep history.
Perhaps we became Romans
a long time ago.
Now - the land still speaks to us -
kisses our skin -

I will not even think the words

Morelle Smith

'It's too hot' - but I do think
of the straw hat for sale -
and wish I'd bought it.
The parasol does not fly off
or come apart.
But every now and then the table
rocks a little, on the cobbles.
The guy at the next table
leans back in his chair,
smiles at me and shuts his eyes.
I wonder what it must feel like
to be the sun
as I lean into the shade.

# Umbra Solis

This unaccustomed sun
slaps light like thick paint
on pavements and metal tables,
windows and mirrors and tucks
shadows, airy napkins -
beneath buildings and eyelids,
bricks and tastes and tongue.

The guardian of shadows
has slipped behind me.
His name lingers in my memory -
in alleyways and evenings
and lack of dark, licking
my shoulders - an embrace
as weighty as a memory.
Absence feels like this
but then - so does
anticipation.

# Langley - Return Journey

Last night's rain
adds a fresh coat of colour
to a morning field of blue flax.
Just off the motorway
gas works, rusted pipes and
power stations and grimy brick walls
form an urban artwork.
Grabs at my heart
as we drive down the miniature streets
trailing whispers
and big memories.

When we leave, we try to pack
them in the boot
beside the books and leaflets,
orange peel, breadcrusts,
paper bags, faded lilac ribbon,
chocolate wrappers, plant pots
and a heap of clothes.
No problem. Everything fits in.

The things we pick up, handle,
stroke, tear off, crumple
and abuse - take up the smallest space.
While the bristly ideas
burst through senses, skin,
fired by imagination,

trailed by memory -
and form whole galaxies of crowded, flaking,
crusted stars that rise and set
rotate and linger -
in quite another place.

# Beachcombing

The rain curtains across
 St. Winwalo's cove.
Green sea churning, thick with the rush
of arrival and ice-crystals -
sugar-coated waves.
Chunks of driftwood.
A heap of tangled octopus rope
and an old green bottle
I persuade my friend to leave behind.

The rain is pulled across the horizon.
Later, we talk of light
and the colours rippling round the body,
like waves of rain.

Shells like thick white plates,
scattered after some sumptuous banquet,
tossed out of the sea.

# Water Barge

Your voice.
It makes a space I can step into
where there is room for me.
It is a journey which holds me,
like the arms of trees.
They bend, they shift slightly,
with the weight, they rock
a little, to accommodate
the fingertips, pressing space
to mould the shapes of words.
When I heard your voice
I knew it was a boat
I could step into; there was
space for me to stretch
my limbs and words; not sink,
but float, on this slow
and gentle barge.

# Beowulf's Going Home

The russet bull leans his head
against the rail.
His pink nose pokes through.
It's the leaning gesture of the head and neck
that draws me to him.

He lies on his yellow straw,
thinking his bull thoughts,
not inclined towards the party,
the coming and going
of minders and owners
and buyers looking
for the length of back,
the girth of rump,
the weight of neck,
while the warbling rattle of the auctioneer
sounds like tinny treble
from the sound system next door.
What a fine bull, ladies, gents,
he's a real bull, who will give me
1,000, 800, he was 3rd prize-winner
at the Royal Show, gents and ladies,
look at him, what a fine bull he is.

No, red/brown Beowulf is not a party animal,
he inclines towards the metal bar
of the pen, he is a weary bull,

a dreaming bull, remembering
the honey grass of home
and the smell of space around him.

I rub his forehead and behind his ears,
while he inclines his head towards me,
shuffles his eyes a little,
deep in thought.
I wonder if this vague feeling
of anguish in me, is something he can feel,
and I would like to shield him
from the knowledge that this slick,
fast-talking auctioneer
is trying to make a sale of him.

He leans against the metal pen
and will not play.
But the salesman isn't getting a high price,
so Beowulf goes home that day,
back to his familiar fields and heifers
and the person who takes care of him
the one who said to me,
as I stroked his ears and head -
oh, that's what he likes, you know,
he cannot get enough of that.

Later, this young man was sitting
on the back of Beowulf, the fair, the brave,
sitting on the soft, brown,
central-heated chair.
As if to say -
he isn't going anywhere today,
Beowulf the bold is coming home.

# Black Cat

Time has slipped back
Into my life a little,
with the dusty cherry blossom
on the pavements,
smells of frying bacon
in early morning cafes.
Time to notice sunlight
hitting black iron railings
so hard, that they bend a little,
curve round buildings,
curl round basement steps;
and there's a cat
in sprawling morning light
leaning its black skin
against them.

# Canal Street Café

The cafe is empty,
except for me, and the person
who brings me a mug of tea.
He is tall, speaks slowly
has a foreign accent I cannot identify
and an exquisite jawline.

Thick moisture on the inside
of the window.
When I run my finger over it,
water drips down the pane.
And outside, it is raining.

A newspaper lies on the table
next to me.
I am writing in my book
and the footsteps of the man
who served me
move slowly across the cafe;
measured steps I hear quite clearly
above the whiny chatter of the radio.
I'm just about to look up
when he picks up the paper,
walks back again
behind the counter.

I left most of the mug of tea,

not because it tasted bad
or I didn't like the mug
or the radio station.
Or because the sound of the knife
being sharpened grated on my ear.
No, I left because I was late for
an appointment.
That's why I didn't drink the tea.
It had nothing to do with that
haunting jawline.

# Crow Poems

## I

Chopin is playing on the radio.
Then a cello slides and tugs
and the last light is just
a pale blue paint above the pine trees.
Chittering of birds
and a dark strip of crow sound.

## II

No frost this morning,
pulling the red and yellow
flowers onto their knees,
plastered with the unforgiving
footsteps of the ice.

We have wind now, rain,
the flower-heads wave and wave
on their arched and crooked stems.
Strange voices in our ears.
And no crow sounds
to silence them.
Then one - stretched and distant
flat-bottomed boat of sound.
My hands curve round the morning.

## III

Morelle Smith

Lying on the grass,
crow sounds are thick ropes
across the sky. I swing from them.
A lyric bird runs through
a repertoire of melodies;
water-streams, a little jig,
a low call, a dance,
a march, a love-song,
a waltz, a hymn.
I laugh out loud.

Little ripples of air kiss my arm.
God - I am reminded -
is this spirit of life
whatever it's clothed in -
grass-stem, warm air,
feathers or fur -
even skin.

# The Fitting

The moon is ovoid
and the hills are shiny-grey -
spider's on the ceiling
and it's coming my way.

Snip snip goes Fate's scissors
and I welcome her in.
She grows young before my eyes,
tawny and wild-haired -
an irreverent child -
friends now, Moon hunters.

Look!  A funnel of sunlight
is rushing towards you.
Not even your wiggly-worm fears
can stop it now.
Already its warm breath is
fanning your face.
Spin-splinter
spin-oyster, sea-bed,
limp starfish,
the octaves of silence -
spin - this race.

Fitting into my skin -
slipping it on like a long,
long sigh of relief -

Morelle Smith

oh my skin, where
have you been all my life?

Tassels of the ash trees, at last,
brushes of leaves fronding the branches,
at last the ash leaves.

# Remembering Giancarlo

*(in memoriam Giancarlo Cesarone)*

He had somewhere that he loved -
I remember, as we drive through
flat country, the sky shuffling
through greys, from diffuse,
to clear, hard edges.
Grey then becomes varieties of nets
to catch the light.
From fishing-nets to fine mesh silk.

He had somewhere that he loved -
a land of blue skies, hot sun,
bright colours and dazzling music.
I remember this, as we drive
through countryside hard as a
beach shell, ridged with memories
of former life.

In some former life it seems
he was interpreter and pharmacist,
but in the one we knew
he brought music from around
the world to a tiny club
in the via Frangipani.
His face folded round his smile
like cupped hands,

dreaming of Africa.

November trees are trelliswork
and scaffolding, outlines and patterns
still to be painted, filled-in.
Waiting for summer and the real thing.

The earth is purple here
and the stone that comes from it,
pinkish-maroon.
We lose a stitch in the loops
of road round Perth,
find it again, drive through Scone
and head for Brechin.

The garden of the alchemist
is lined with plum-red stone.
The sky is apple-thick,
with a plume of elderberry.
Stone carvings line the walls -
Sol and Luna, Musica and Geometria.
Hedges are trimmed into
letters - messages of hope.
Hedges that spell. Tended,
cut, shaped into Latin words.
Dum spiro spero.
I think about the gardener.
And the patience and precision and the love.

The cold wind felt like grit
being rubbed against the skin.

He had somewhere that he loved.
Dream or hope, vision or future -
perhaps it kept him going

pushed him on or held him back,
I do not know.

The well, set in the south wall
shows a circle of light
at the bottom. If your sight
was good enough, you could see
your own face, peering over the
stone rim, looking at the water
and reflected light.

Dusk comes slowly in the garden
of the alchemist,
with its stone carved luminaries,
deities and Arts
and its coded message, in hedge-script -
Dum spiro spero,
reminding us that life and dream
life and hope and vision -
they belong together.
I'm remembering Giancarlo
and his dream of Africa
as I close the gate behind me
to the garden of
the alchemist.

Morelle Smith

# Identity

Yellow light on the ash leaves.
Last night I heard the owl,
and this morning too.
I will wear soft colours, I resolve,
lilac, sea-green, blue
as distance, the blue
that memory is made of.

There are only moments
when we even glimpse
all of what we are.
Sometimes we give them faces,
names and we say -
stay with us -
and the form stays, and the moment
slips away from us
like a blurred moth
through the morning trees.

How do you track the moment?
A line of light thread,
across the rose leaves.
You offer it the space
to breathe in you.
Entice it in.
You remember that it wants
to live within you, always.

You remember that its home
is in you, you remember -
that it's you.
Remember - who you are.

# The Sculptor's Garden

*(for Lesley-May Miller)*

At some point, everything turns into something else.
In the sculptor's garden, ceramic leaves
appear among the hedges,
green-veined, laced with words.
A stone figure, lightly-shrouded, leans towards
the blue-green waves of some pine-needled sea,
another has arms lifted, like a dancer.

There are maps drawn onto parchment-yellow
clay stones, on the path.
I lift my feet, kneel down, to read.
On one, there is a dancing Shiva,
words like 'jasmine' and 'layer of belief'
and these, for me, turn into something else.

After that, there are huge leaves
of a plant whose name I can't remember,
reminding me of blue-tinged fig leaves,
grasses with delicate, hanging fronds,
a path marked 'passage protege',
and apple trees, a book
made out of copper leaves.

'This figure stood before an arch,
a gateway to another world,' the sculptor said.

'But the arch has leaned into the hedge,
so now she's through the archway,
she's in the other world.'
Everything has shifted slightly,
as if I too, have gone beyond the arch
that leads into the other world.

Driving home, Tagore's words,
written on the Shiva stone, turn into minarets,
and I am seized with longing
for the undulating song of prayer,
which then turns into an image
of someone's thick black hair, dark eyes,
and laughter running through his body.
He has turned into the archway
and the gate, a mosaic of all memories
like fig-leaves and minarets, the jasmine scents,
the pale green sea; all these he
encapsulates, as well as all the memories
that are still to come, that wait,
sheltered in the archways and the wings
of Time; waiting for the meeting
we have only dreamed about.

Everything, at some point, turns into something else.
The dark-haired man is not the future's keeper,
but in my mind, he curves towards me
like an arch - and time presses,
like a drum rhythm, on my ears and skin,
shaking, shaking me, to follow
in this rhythm's footsteps,
and walk towards the future,
with measured steps, while my senses
and my vision and my heart, all these
are telling me to run.

Outwardly calm, I walk through the
garden's journey - 'past is present
in this garden' says one ceramic leaf.
The 'passage protege' I step over
tugs me into future, prised open
by the jasmine leaves, and minarets
and promises of figs to come.

At some point, everything turns into something else,
and I am following this rhythm,
like a signpost, like a map,
like an impatient dream
that's on its way to meet me.
I recognize the future's drum-beat.
It's slipped inside me,
and become the rhythm of my heart.

# In the Jazz Café

It's just beginning to get dark
and a blackbird sings of spring
in the courtyard of Blackfriars.
The air is still, speckled with night
and the January blackbird
sings of spring.

In the Jazz Cafe,
Brenda buys a bottle of red wine
and the owner passes us two tumblers
from behind the bar.
Someone sitting at a table opposite
has an earring and dark hair
and smiles to his companions.

We go home in the pebbled dark,
past the Monument,
and the Italian cafe
and the shopping centre
wind rustling the garbage bags
and throwing paper
and pizza boxes across the road.
The streets are damp and solitary,
warm and windy
for the time of year.

The young man in the Jazz Cafe

whose smile did not reach my table
reminded me of Jen, with his earring
and his green eyes.
Jen lives in Delmare Street
and to reach his house
I took the pedestrian bridge
that crosses the railway
and gives you a view of the sea.
When I said I'd best be going
he said yes, you'd better.
That was what he said. And then -
'Otherwise I'd keep you here forever.'
I picked up my books and bag.
Put on my jacket
wondering where the words might be
to say - I'd like to change my mind
and stay - and really, it's OK for you
to keep me here forever.

But there's never space for words like that
and so I leave and walk up Delmare Street,
its old stone houses,
gardens in the front, with summer roses
trailing scent and smells of cut grass
mingling with the salt air of the sea
which I catch a glimpse of
when I turn around.

Falling in love with city streets
is a hazard only if you miss
the boundary between the pavement
and the road, dividing line between
protective, tended gardens
and the highways with signs like -
'To the Predators Path' or -

'Lane of Utter Loneliness' or -
'Last Refuge of the Heart' or -
'There's Still Time to Get Off This Highway'.
Open road or tended garden,
which is the more lethal
of the two?

I made a narrow escape
I tell myself, no mistake about it
as I turn around and there's the grey sea
on horizon and a whiff of salt.
I cross the bridge
over the railway and wake up
in the morning with an ache
between my shoulder blades
as if I had carried something heavy
on my back for a long long time.

I spent the summer
trying to shrug it off,
kept myself busy painting walls
and hanging pictures at the exhibition.
I grew precise and intimate
with folds of muslin, staple guns
and velvet hangings that I stroked
with vague nostalgia I couldn't place
until Jen walked inside one day
and I ran my fingers carelessly
across his head and the soft fur
of his hair reminded me -
of velvet. Not that I had ever touched
his hair before, but I should
have known - I don't know
what exactly but there was this
strong sensation in my fingers

telling me I now knew something
that I should have known before.

Jen takes me two blocks down the street
where we rescue an abandoned chair
and bring it back with us,
to the exhibition.
He has tattoos, one earring,
a sheaf of papers and a ball of stories
that he can't unwind.
He looks at me for clues
and I know I must abandon, now,
my pretence of counsellor, of objectivity,
of older sister who knows
all the answers, for I have none,
just this gesture of my fingers
moving through his hair.

Soon after that, he leaves
and when the exhibition closes
I take the chair home.
As we dismantle velvet, muslin,
nails and the branches, stones,
shells and tapestries and sculptures
from the window,
there is a chill, a shiver
in the grey air, that was
not there before.

It was not there in the early morning
sunshine kissing the flagstones
and the fronts of buildings
when we opened the doors,
spread butter on croissants
and gave coffee and wine to our friends,

and when he came he brought
the salted sea air with him
and pieces of a story he kept trying
to tell me, while I put more coffee
in the filter, poured out cups,
added sugar, handed them out,
spread butter on croissants,
got some on my finger, licked it
and looked at him -

and he said -
'I travelled to Iona' -
'And met an albatross, was that it?'
I spoke crossly, for it was clear
that he'd been stung by miracles
and he kept finding his way back to me,
needing me to hear his story.
'Well, I hope you didn't kill it.'

Me, I was just jealous
and he grinned at me
and I caught pieces of his story,
among the croissant crumbs
and sugar cubes and milk cartons
and wine bottles and the bracelets
of my friends and the bright colours
that they wore and the talk
and the hanging pictures,
glinting in the sunlight
sloping and slinking through the open door.

But when we said goodbye to the
nasturtiums leaning their soft
orange petals on the ledge
outside the window -

goodbye to the downy folds of
muslin on the walls
and the snakes of gold thread in the hangings,
the sky was parcelled up
tight, in its drawstring bag of cloud
and the air snipped its chilly teeth
at us.

I still have the chair we found
abandoned in the street -
I also have phone messages
and cards and promises to meet up -
soon - and - I see someone in the Jazz Cafe
and I remember
smells of sea and cut grass,
the green eyes, the feel of velvet
as I stroke his hair; crossing the bridge
over the railway line, crossing the threshold,
out into the street -
'You'd better go, otherwise
I'll keep you here forever.'

Falling in love with city streets
and tended gardens
and the scent of roses -
and choosing the highway -
What stays forever anyway?
I say to Brenda, as she
pours more wine and I watch
the young man with the earring
laughing, in the Jazz Cafe.
'Some memories do, I guess,'
she says.

# Kairos Time

The moment, slowing at the roundabout,
birdsong slanting in the window,
with the sunlight - a weight
is lifted and a door swings open
into a time-free world.

I change gear. Move away.
This this, it seems to say
in this moment on the lip
between the worlds -
between fixation and forgetting
and the terse and tangled dialogue
between them -
this is the belonging
that you seek so endlessly,
so fixedly, so fearfully,
eyes tight wrapped
around a future that the blackbird
spills, along with sunlight,
through a crevice, just a chink
in your attention -
relaxing the fever and the fear.

Layers of time are stacked in me
like bricks.
Driving on the wet-skinned road
I realise it isn't memories

that free us.
It's release of them
that vanishes the hard, skin-bruising edges
of the layers of brick -
it's release of them,
that lets love in.

# The Language of Dream

You can't bite it
or taste it,
can't feel the melted butter
soaked into the bread,
can't smell the damp flower
salty scent of skin
beside your own.
'cheese and pickle on both sides
then folded to make a sandwich'
says the boy next door,
to his father.
Through my open door,
I can smell the roasting
cheese on toast,
hear the clatter of cups,
banging of cupboards.

Coming home last night,
I heard the oyster catcher cries,
and, sitting in the garden,
in the half dark of a summer night
I heard little sounds
half coughs, half sneezes
but no sounds of movement.
This must be the way
a hedgehog dreams, I thought,
the sighs and snuffles

of a flying creature
that has left its prickly
skin behind.

No, in dream's language
you will not see the scraps
of casual white
a butterfly dances against green,
or the horizontal flight
of finch.

You will use the muscles
of your feelings
to take you high above
the hills close to Moon
and pine tree tops.
You will connect via the routes
the longing heart,
unleashed at last,
follows in freedom -
with its free passage
through times and worlds,
unpeeling masks, revealing
what is there and was and always
will be.
It isn't far, the journey
that they claim is light-years
long, this star-path,
travelled on a ship
with heart as helmsman,
face hidden in the dark,
a shadowy figure
that you wanted to be with
and had forgotten just how much
you wanted -

no, it takes no longer
this way, than the
surfacing of your desire
to be there -

The language of the dream
will turn your head,
change your perception,
like a painting -
and if you listen to its words
there will still be room
for butterflies and
cheese on bread
and oyster catcher cries
and sleeping hedgehogs
and the smell of newly-woken skin
washed like a canvas
in pale morning light.

# In Night's Hands

The night has crept in close,
Trailed indolent indigo across the sky,
Reaches out its black hands
As I step out of the bookstore,
Guides me along the street
As if I was blind before
And only now am capable of following
The night.

'Black absorbs all frequencies'
The young man says,
The bright metal button
Gleaming in his ear.
'The colour red for example,
Has absorbed all other frequencies
Of light apart from red.
Red is what it reflects.'
So a red thing is seen as red
Precisely because red
Is what it is not.

The night absorbs all colours.
Stuffed full of colours,
Pockets bursting, mouth crammed
Full as Squirrel's, taking nuts
From source to larder.
Night treads softly, slowly,

Through the streets.
I clasp its black hands
For I know now, that however
Full of light they'll be
It still cannot refuse me,
Even with its brimful hands
There will still be room for me,
Inside the night.

# Light

Pools and patches of water
on the wooden benches
in the outside courtyard.
It must have rained this morning.
Even outside feels like
being inside somewhere else,
where the heat has been turned on
and forgotten,
and the dimmer turned to 'sultry'.

This kind of light will not change
its angle or its density,
it will give no indication
of shift, movement, no clues at all
as to morning or late evening
just these bars of light
that switch time like an egg
removing masks and roles,
plans and diets and the ordinary
consequences; different times
bump into one another,
overlap, running into past and
future, the way water
finds its way to different levels.

Days unfold - like blankets,
like parcel tape and outer wrappings,

coloured paper, soft tissue -
usually they do.
In ordered sequence, as the sun,
and all its followers of light -
proceed.

But this day the sundial is empty
and the shadows are silent.
Beginning and end met somewhere
in secret and vowed
never to be parted again.
The game of time steps -
ascending, returning, is losing
its hold and its glamour.
I want to shift gear into non-time,
slip the net,
feel precarious walking on slopes,
melt into images, any images
in this grey/silver light
will do,
waxed and polished,
all images are made of this
non-time, grey/green sheen
that I can claim and own
and say belongs to me,
because it is me,
and the light and I clasp hands
across the table.

We reach for moments like this,
reach and stretch and wrestle
sometimes with the one whose face
wears the mask of love we put on them.
They ought to give us
the experience of intimacy we once

found with them, then lost.
Surely they are holding back, have
stashed it in some cupboard,
keeping us from it?
But no matter how we weep and flail
or hurl abuse, it isn't there.
They do not possess it,
we have lost it, somehow.
Loss replaces moments of
no measurement, no space, no time.

I flip the straw in the coke can
and the coffee grows tepid, then bitter.
There is a slight movement of air.
The newspaper flaps a warning corner.
The air is clammy, but fresh too,
with the slight wind.
The air is pancake flat
on the top of my head,
on my friend's sea-green dress.

Loss is not the worst of company,
if you learn its secrets
and its nature and the things
it has to say.
Loss has many memories and stories,
comes to fit you like a dream.
Then one day you hear it
singing in the early light,
one evening the scent of honeysuckle
takes your breath away.
Loss turns into Presence
and you find it in a day
of flat light, entering your heart
where there is no space

no time, no boundaries at all.

I take a last sip of the coffee,
I am solitary in the courtyard
now; and dazzled by the hat
of light; the kiss of air
on skin, damp patches
on the bench and table
and the tipping of the heart
that monochrome can give you,
with its shades and subtlety
resembling the heart's gestures,
curve of hand, shadow of
jawline, wave of shoulder
flowing into arm.

In the kingdom of the heart
there are no boundaries,
no wars, no spies, no enemy
patrols and no suspicion.
And most of all, no kings.
But you are there, your own self -
solitary -
drenched with light.

# Left Luggage

A curl of silver chocolate -
a nail-paring of light
next to Venus, in the smooth sky
the celestial painter
has dripped on
leaving some smudged - and some dried -
pinpricks and dribbles of light.

Until I feel my feet
so securely on the path
that they fall in love with
the ground they walk on,
all these pretty men
will be deviation, impasses,
strada senza uscita,
left luggage of the psyche,
lost property office of the mind.

# Mettle Worker

The wind soars through the trees,
armed with fantasies, flurried
with feathers, an armoury of
cool breath, licking the skin
into light. Pausing,
then hurtling through the soft,
new leaves.
They will become tough
and weather-tested and dark green.
They will become the bass line
of summer. A drum beat.
But every season now
feels fleeting. Never still.
Never anchored, always tugging
for some change, some other road,
hankering for future.
Just like love.

Or as it sometimes comes to us -
arriving in a whirl of light -
and passion and pink blossom on pavements -
scattering us like those discarded shells -
tipping easy answers from our tongue,
ripping out floorboards of our
inept and clumsy carpentry.
Hephaestus, your crippled limbs
give rise to marvels.

Morelle Smith

Teach me your skill -
patience, and love of your art
and an ear to listen to the dying
of the wind, in the dark garden,
shimmering with life.
And teach me most of all, Hephaestus,
to remember who I am,
whether there is wind or rain
or stillness, in the night garden.

# Night Bus

The bus glides and swings
through the night streets
of the city; it is
almost empty, this brightly-lit
well-heated, near-deserted
boat of a bus, swinging
through the dim night-streets,
the quiet, cobbled back-streets
of the city; full of silence
and secrets, so familiar -
the slow, waltzing, rocking
barn of a bus takes me
through these streets
which I love with a night
passion, a hugging, bursting
secret of a love,
tucked in my inside pocket,
next to my heart.

This stately secret of a bus,
ablaze with lights;
love is a slow journey
through night streets
lit with cool white lights -
not a person or possession
but a cupped tangle of images -
remembering her eyes

dark as the indigo
in pools between the street lights,
a gesture of the hand through hair,
the compass on the tiled floor,
and a white moon leaping in the sky,
framed in the open door
as we step out into the night.

Then this slow and rocking journey
showing my life to me
in dreaming streets
and gleaming lights.
Night journey
through a dream of coming home.

# Night Out

The mist seeps and slips into gardens,
houses and thoughts.
A soft blindness, a hood of memories,
a wall of distance, a creeping longing,
a jolt of uncertainty, a trickle of light.

The night is spread, like butter,
like salve over a wound.
Sleep now, gentle beetles, birds,
stars and grounded aeroplanes
in quiet, empty sheds,
dark woods and burrows.
Nights of shadows are too full of life
for timid humans.
But I leave the window open
to let the dreams come in.

Morelle Smith

# Paradox

There was always a no
tucked inside my yes,
like the dot of yin
in yang.

In this world of yes and no
there is always one who takes
the turn of shadow,
slips out of focus,
is content to watch, to listen,
push wolfish dreams through
barely open windows;
pause at the left,
while you turn to the right.

In the night perhaps,
the shadows come out from the wings,
draw us into a drama
we may not care to claim
or recognise as ours
tossing emotions at us as if life
was just a game of catch -
a ballgame - catch and throw
it back - catch and miss -
it hits you in the belly
and you gasp for air -
catch and -

fall.
You don't feel in control
in this game.
Not in control at all.

In the world of yes and no
I often feel that there
is someone at my shoulder -
watching me or prompting me -
tricking me or pushing me.
An adversary, skilled at subterfuge,
a Loki figure, harmless
trickster with his bag of charms
and dice; clad in skins,
a wintry figure - eyes like ice.
But when I turn around
there is no-one there behind me -
just my own reflection
in the plate glass window -
looking more stern and severe
and more determined than I ever
thought I looked.

How can I trust this watcher
when I do not know what tricks
he might play on me,
what dream scenarios he might invent
and draw me into?
How do I become skilled at
the game of ball, the art
of juggling when I cannot
even guess the rules
of a world outside of
boundaries and marker-posts -
a rimless world, unperimetered

and unseduced by time.

It's when I realise I cannot know,
cannot control
what the future's going to be
that I let go of resistance,
take this unfamiliar hand -
so dangerous in its ability
to topple the fine balance
of my safe, familiar world -
and recognise this other -
that pauses at the left
while I turn to the right -
part-time adversary,
part-time love -
is looking for it's long-lost
other self -
in me.

# Splitman

I am the split man,
I walk with a limp
and I have something on my shoulder
you can see perhaps
but I - I cannot bear
to look at it.

My wound is not the subject
of dinner party conversation.
And so I sleep in porches,
barns, if I am lucky,
abandoned old buildings,
that no-one else wants.

I know you do not like
to look me in the eye
although I can - at times -
be useful - fixing a broken fence,
mending a torn coat -
my needlework is neat as any woman's,
I can turn my hand to almost anything
I say - almost.

One day a young girl asked me in,
stretched out her hand to me -
I said I could not stay
only - if I can do something in return

only if I can pay my way
with service.
She said nothing.

When I think back sometimes
I wonder - was it because
she did not know the words
for what I could do for her?
Was it something less familiar
to her than shoes to be mended,
hedges to be cut,
leaves to be raked?
And if the words do not exist,
does that mean that the
inarticulate, which cannot speak
for itself, which is dumb
and silent - as our feelings are -
does it not exist as well?

Do our feelings always need a shelter?
Do they always need a covering
of words to wear,
before they can exist at all?

I am a tramp
and any shelter I can find
is always borrowed,
temporary, loaned to me.
But sometimes I feel I have a home,
or could have -
when I remember that young girl,
I think that -
if there is anywhere I could call home
it's in that unclothed, silent space
when it appeared that there

was nothing I could do for her -
or nothing she could say.
And I don't suppose
I'll ever know now,
because I turned away.

I'm getting older now
older, less useful,
uglier and more distasteful.
I would like to go back
to that time
when I was offered something
that did not have a name.
Maybe I will one day.
Is it possible to reel back time?
For if it was
I would stop it at that moment -
the child's brown hair,
the singing birds,
the sunlight on the grass and trees,
to all these wordless things
and the feelings rising in me
yes, I'd listen to what
the feelings had to say.

# Urban Angel

It is night time.
I do not know the place
where we are going, but to reach it
we are heading for the centre of the city.
There is no other way.
There is no by-pass or ring-road,
no beltway or peripherique
to avoid the grime and detritus,
the stale, sweat-coated city air.
Oh no, I say, don't, driver,
take me into the city's broken heart,
have pity on me,
I do not choose to go there.
But he drives on,
as if he did not hear.

There are shacks made up
of broken bits of tin,
cracked through with rain and wind.
There are cardboard houses,
buckling with damp;
people living on refuse heaps,
people living nowhere,
sleeping under bridges
and in doorways,
sodden blankets to protect
them from the cold.

There are people with no eyes,
people with missing limbs -

Don't show me any more!
I cry, to the driver's back.
I do not know him,
have not seen his face,
who is this man who takes me
on this journey to the underworld,
the sub-zone of the city?
When I cannot bear the images
of suffering, I let out
a long cry and he exhales,
as if he feels relief.

I am weeping, in the sub-world
of the city and he stops the car,
turns round.
And it seems to me I know him
and have always known him.
Every face I've ever loved
is in that face.
And the light from him
is like a blanket round me,
like a pair of wings that hold me -
always - never letting go.

Why did you leave me? I ask him.
Why were you not always here with me?
Why did you turn your back on me
and leave me in this dark
and maimed place,
with only streetlights
and car headlights in the night?
Why show me all this suffering,

which is too great
for my heart to bear?

Though he does not speak,
I know the answers - coming from him,
rising up in me.
There was no abandonment,
only forgetting.
There was no darkness,
only the shadow of my fear.
And there is no reconciliation
until the wound of our forgetting
revives in us a longing
to be who we really are.
And that longing, that emotion
ends the separation,
brings us home.

# The Messenger

I imagined him in all my dreams.
The work we'd do together
from our common purpose,
and the places we would travel.
The way the waters of all rivers
we would walk beside -
The Seine, Arno, Tevere
Danube and Drin -
would reflect sunlight
and penetrate our skin.

He passed the dream on to me,
like a carrier, a messenger
with something vital to impart.
It travelled up my spine
gave me entry to a world
that is difficult to access,
even after years of searching.
It took - perhaps a few seconds
but I wasn't counting at the time
I was slipping past the sentry posts
and entering a world
I'd always wanted to be in.

The secret of getting in is very simple.
It involves discarding all pretences,
all masks, all coverings

protections and defences
and revealing your real self,
which is made of love,
a vulnerable matter
in this world of edges
and bartering and commerce
with an eye for gain
and a calculating tongue
and where the heart feels
an outsider -
excluded and unwanted,
and has lost the password -
or never had it anyway -
has forgotten why it came here,
since the business of the world
is not its business -
and looks to find a way
of being its real self
and
of being in the world.

I didn't know at first,
he was a messenger -
I just liked the way
he seemed to carry something in him
and even though he talked about
his past, his plans and purposes,
there was something in him
that he didn't give away.

It was only afterwards
I thumbed through memories,
looking for codes and clues,
keys and answers,
most of all, answers

as if his tongue had pushed
a folded piece of paper
between my lips
and on it was the scribbled
missing part of the equation.

It was not, of course, in words,
it was the moment, in itself,
that was the answer -
the moment when all armour
was relinquished, all the
guards had left and in the middle
of this world of commerce,
currency and calculation,
the real nature of my being
poured into my consciousness
like light.

Like light reflected from the surface
of the Seine, the Danube,
the Sava or the Drin.

We fill this bag of light
with contents from our dreams
like eager pilgrims
setting out to find
the river's source or destination,
quest-hungry, with as
light a load as possible.

We fill in destinations
like request slips for leave
of absence from our work.
I don't know the co-ordinates
of passage and arrival.

I hazard guesses mostly
and often get the answers
wrong; but the places
I end up in and the people
that I find there,
they are always right.

So we haven't worked together
or walked by any of these rivers
but that doesn't matter.
What matters is that moment
and its memory
and the seed of light I carry
with me, the desire
to seek out unknown paths
discover ways and tracks
that will be reached, always,
by a different route, the terrain
always unknown, so we
have to be supremely present
and with no protection
other than our trust.

A place where once again the messenger
might push the folded paper,
with his tongue,
between your lips.
Not that you will think
about the paper
with his tongue licking your lips -

Whatever meetings you will not have
or you will have, in the future,
you will always love
the messenger

for that moment when
the message and the bearer -
like the dancer and the dance -
become one and the same.